# Non-Fiction and Fiction Writing for 7–11 years

# IGNITING WRITING

# 3

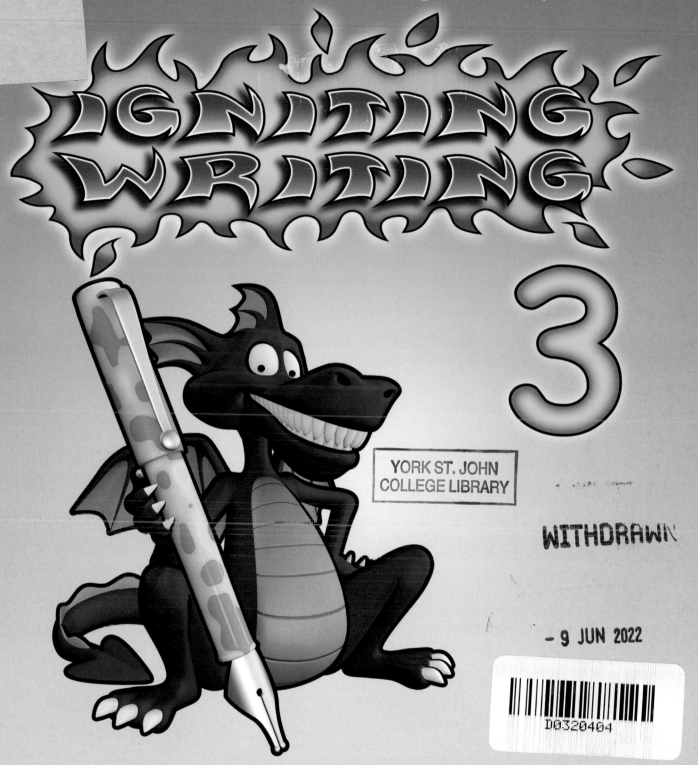

YORK ST. JOHN
COLLEGE LIBRARY

WITHDRAWN

– 9 JUN 2022

D0320404

## Pie Corbett • Sue Palmer • Ann Webley

Nelson Thornes
a Wolters Kluwer business

York St John

3 8025 00505466 6

Text © Sue Palmer, Pie Corbett and Nelson Thornes  2006

Original illustrations © Nelson Thornes Ltd 2006

The right of Pie Corbett and Sue Palmer to be identified as authors of this work has been asserted by them in accordance with the Copyright, Designs and Patents Act 1988.

All rights reserved. No part of this publication may be reproduced or transmitted in any form or by any means, electronic or mechanical, including photocopy, recording or any information storage and retrieval system, without permission in writing from the publisher or under licence from the Copyright Licensing Agency Limited, of 90 Tottenham Court Road, London W1T 4LP.

Any person who commits any unauthorised act in relation to this publication may be liable to criminal prosecution and civil claims for damages.

Published in 2006 by:
Nelson Thornes Ltd
Delta Place
27 Bath Road
CHELTENHAM
GL53 7TH
United Kingdom

06 07 08 09 10 / 10 9 8 7 6 5 4 3 2 1

A catalogue record for this book is available from the British Library

ISBN 0 7487 9731 9

Illustrations by Tom Bamfield and Can Studios
Page make-up by Pantek Arts, Maidstone, Kent

Printed in Croatia by Zrinski

# Contents

# Introduction

The *Igniting Writing* sequences will help you learn more about writing. When you are working independently this book will help you to:

- think about what to include

- plan your work

- decide how to organise your writing in sections or paragraphs

- choose the right sorts of words and sentences for the kind of writing you are doing

- edit and improve your work when you have finished.

## Contents of the CDs

| CD 1: Journeys | |
| --- | --- |
| **Sequence** | **Text type** |
| **Theme: Quests** | |
| Story of a Quest<br>Dispatches from a Quest<br>Scenes from a Quest | Story<br>Letter writing<br>Playscript |
| **Theme: Jets** | |
| The Jet Engine<br>Air Safety<br>Jet Travel: Good or Bad? | Explanation<br>Instructions<br>Persuasion (L) Discussion (U) |
| **Theme: Pilgrimages** | |
| The Annual Hajj<br>Hindu Pilgrimages<br>A Visit to Jerusalem | Diary<br>Poetry<br>Recount |
| **Theme: Space Travel** | |
| Guide to the Planet Marco<br>Outer Space, Outer Mind<br>Finding Blue | Report<br>Website/Advert<br>Science fiction story |

| CD 2: Waterworlds | |
| --- | --- |
| **Sequence** | **Text type** |
| **Theme: Titanic** | |
| The Biggest and Best<br>The Sinking of the Titanic<br>Water, Ice and Reflections | Information text<br>Newspaper report<br>Poetry |
| **Theme: Shipwreck!** | |
| Diary of a Cabin Boy<br>Shipwreck!<br>Water Cycle | Diary<br>Narrative<br>Explanation (U) |
| **Theme: Atlantis** | |
| Atlantis – a Perfect World<br>The Search for Atlantis<br>Atlantis Found! | Brochure<br>Story<br>Playscript |
| **Theme: Creatures of the Deep** | |
| The Great White Shark<br>Dolphins – Our Best Friend?<br>Does the Loch Ness Monster Exist? | Report<br>Persuasion<br>Discussion |

# Writing fiction

To make it easier for you to use this book, the different aspects of fiction writing are broken down into separate sections. Good writers, however, weave together all they know about character, setting and plot, and may even give you information about all three in the same sentence.

Look carefully at the extract below.

> Danny Watson hung onto the side of <u>My Dream</u> and squinted across the vast expanse of the Mediterranean Sea.
>
> 'How much longer are we going to be?' he whined.
>
> 'I reckon we're close,' his father replied, ignoring his son's bad mood. 'This is it lads!'
>
> The excitement was clear in Rob Watson's voice.
>
> 'Loads of people have tried to find the Lost City of Atlantis but no one has succeeded – until now.'

Key:  Information about character
      Information about setting
      Information about plot

Can you see how the writer has threaded together the elements of story writing in this short extract? Dialogue is used to move the plot forward, but it also tells you about the characters and the setting. The characters' actions move the plot forwards, but also reveal their personalities. The setting is integral to this story, as it sets the scene for an adventure or suspense story.

Different types of stories will emphasise different aspects of story writing. An action/adventure/suspense story, like the one above, will probably use a lot of dialogue. A story about issues or characters' feelings may focus more on how the main character feels. A fantasy or science fiction story would probably give more detail about the setting. Think carefully about the type of story you are writing, and the effect that you want your writing to have, as you craft your work.

Finally, all good writers edit their stories. Always go back to your work and take time to improve it.

# Characters

## Getting ideas

Think of someone that you know, have seen or met. Use this as a basis for creating a new character; take someone you know and then change something about them. You can also use pictures, look through newspapers and magazines and cut out possible characters.

1. Decide on a name.

   - Choose a name to reflect your character, e.g. *Weasel*.
   - Use names that suggest character.

2. Think of a few details to describe your character. This will help the reader be able to 'see' the character.

   - 'Futuristic' clothing suggests a science fiction or fantasy story.
   - 'Red trainers' suggests someone lively and adventurous.

3. Decide how your character is feeling, e.g.

   > upset, lonely, brave, helpful, curious, adventurous

## Building your character

- Use others' reactions and comments, e.g. *Zak hid outside by the water tower, his teacher's sarcastic voice still ringing in his ears. He stood and gulped back the tears.*

- Give your character an interest or sport, e.g. *Numbers meant nothing to Zak. He'd never be a space pilot now …*

- Reveal your character's thoughts, e.g. *He was bound to fail his space tests.*

- Show how the story changes them, e.g. *Zak gulped. Maybe the space tests would not be too hard after all …*

- Contrast the opening and ending.

- At the end, show what the characters have learned.

- Show events from different characters' viewpoints, e.g. *His mother had warned him against going near anything that looked strange, but instinctively, Zak knew that it was a friendly gesture.*

## WRITER'S TOOLKIT

To develop your characters, ask questions about them:

✔ How old are they?

✔ What are they interested in?

✔ Do they have anything they really dislike?

✔ Have they a special talent?

✔ Do they have a secret?

✔ What are they afraid of?

## LANGUAGE TOOLKIT

What do your characters look like?

✔ Use one or two **details**, e.g. *Then the creature blinked its large, blue eyes and made a soft humming noise. It held out its hand, stretching a bony finger towards Zak.*

✔ Describe with a **list**, e.g. *It gurgled contentedly, gave a low hum of pleasure and its body turned from grey to blue!*

✔ Use well-chosen **adjectives**.

✔ Use **similes**, e.g. *Its hot, dry skin pressed against him like autumn leaves.*

Show how they feel through what they say.

✔ Reflect their **personality/feelings**, e.g. 'Let me help you.'

✔ Use powerful **speech verbs**, e.g. *he* <u>whispered</u>.

✔ Use 'said' plus an **adverb**, e.g. *he said* <u>calmly</u>.

✔ Use typical **expressions**, e.g. 'Oh, rats!'

✔ Avoid a string of dialogue.

Show how they feel by what they do.

✔ Use powerful **verbs**, e.g. *it* <u>slouched</u>

✔ Use **adverbs**, e.g. <u>Tentatively</u>, *he stretched out a finger …*

# Settings

1. **What sort of story are you going to write?**
Before you can think about creating a setting, you need to think about the type of story you are writing. Make a list of possible settings.

2. **Where do I begin?**
   - **Picture it:** Try using a photograph, picture or drawing to help with thinking about the setting. Label the picture with descriptive words or phrases. Remember that your reader will not see the picture, so use details and be precise.
   - **Draw it:** Draw a map or landscape of your story setting. This is a good way of creating a setting for a fantasy or sci-fi story.
   - **Sense it:** Close your eyes and imagine you are standing in your setting. What can you hear, smell and feel? What time of day is it? What is the weather like?
   - **Film it:** Imagine you are filming your setting. What can you see through the lens? How does the perspective change as you zoom in to focus on details, or pan out to see the whole scene?

   - **Now write it:**

     Sanctus stared out across the rocks towards the reef. He could still see the remains of the ship's hull poking out of the water like an old sheep's ribs. Waves smashed on the shoreline. Some of the sailors were searching for anything that had been washed up overnight. They looked like crows picking at the sand, caught in the wind's teeth. It had been three days since the shipwreck – three days of cold wind and rain. Three days of misery.

### Remember!
Weave the setting description into the story by linking it to how the characters feel and what they do and say. Change the setting to create a different mood. To create suspense use a lonely, dark setting.

## WRITER'S TOOLKIT

✔ Choose an interesting name for your setting.

✔ Picture it; use places you know and use your imagination.

✔ Think about the time of day and weather.

✔ For different settings, use interesting details.

✔ Show the setting through the main character's eyes, e.g. Sam looked at ...

✔ Use unexpected detail as a 'hook', e.g. one window was broken ...

✔ Change settings to alter the mood and create atmosphere,
e.g. comfy – the kitchen was warm; scary – the alley was dark and cold.

## LANGUAGE TOOLKIT

Have you used:

✔ a **list** to build a picture, e.g.
He saw a tall tower, distant fir trees and snow-capped mountains

✔ **adjectives** to describe, e.g.
the <u>cold stone</u> steps

✔ **adverbs**, e.g.
<u>Silently</u>, the trees whispered

✔ powerful **verbs**, e.g.
snow <u>swirled</u>

✔ **similes**, e.g.
frozen <u>like</u> <u>a</u> <u>mirror</u>

✔ **metaphors**? e.g.
<u>stony rain</u> fell

# Creating plots

## Getting ideas

A good storywriter is always on the lookout for a story idea. You need a story built around a 'problem'. You might get ideas from:

- stories that you have read
- story tapes
- retelling or changing traditional tales, nursery rhymes or story poems
- things that happen to you
- anecdotes.

Start by mixing together your ingredients:

- **Who** is the main character?
- **Where** is he/she?
- **What** is he/she doing?
- **What** is going to go wrong?
- **How** will it be sorted out?
- **How** will it end?

## Story patterns

It can help if you use a basic pattern for your writing. To see a list of different types of stories, plus their plot features, look on page 23. Here are some suggestions for basic plot ideas:

- overcoming a problem
- quest/journey
- conquer the monster
- character flaw
- warning
- lost/found
- suspense
- wishing

- catastrophe
- magical
- stories with a moral
- changing (sad – happy, poor – rich, weak over strong, good over evil)
- traditional pattern.

## How to plan

Start jotting down ideas for the plot. Think about what will happen next, but keep the plot simple and clear. Here are some useful planning tools for different types of stories.

### Flowcharts

A flowchart is ideal for planning a play or a story that takes place in different settings.

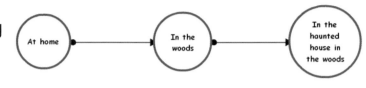

### Timelines

A timeline is helpful for planning a letter or a diary. It allows you to put events in chronological order.

### Storyboards

A storyboard is a good way of planning if you like to map out how each scene will look. It allows you to use a combination of words and pictures to plan out your story.

### Story picture maps

You might find a story picture map useful if you are writing a science fiction or fantasy story. It enables you to create the setting and the plot together, in a visual way.

### Story mountain

Use a story mountain to build excitement or interest into your storyline. A good plot should have moments of suspense or crisis, or the characters should be faced with a problem or challenge.

## WRITER'S TOOLKIT

Have you:

✔ used your plan to help you write your story

✔ made any changes, and have they added to your original idea

✔ controlled the dialogue, or is there too much

✔ balanced the action, dialogue and description

✔ made the story well-paced or have you rushed any part

✔ shown what the main character is like by what they say and do

✔ written an ending that shows how the main character feels or what has been learned?

## LANGUAGE TOOLKIT

Have you:

✔ stayed in the same **tense**

✔ stayed in the same **person**, e.g. I, or *he/she*

✔ used connectives to link ideas, sentences and make paragraph changes?

e.g.   Once upon a time; One day; Suddenly, so, Finally

---

### Remember!

Different story types may use different patterns, e.g.
- traditional — patterns of three (three tasks, three brothers)
- sci-fi — good versus evil invaders
- adventure — defeating robbers or kidnappers.

Muddling story types can create comedy, e.g. rewriting *Little Red Riding Hood* as a thriller.

# Writing dialogue

## WRITER'S TOOLKIT

✔ Think about what sort of thing each character would say.

✔ Think about who is speaking and how they are feeling.

✔ Use the dialogue to move the action forwards, e.g. 'Let's climb the tree,' said Shasta.

✔ Have characters discussing events.

✔ Listen to the sorts of things people say and steal ideas!

✔ Collect expressions.

✔ Show what a character is doing while they speak by adding information, e.g. 'Look,' said Shasta, showing everyone the stones.

## LANGUAGE TOOLKIT

✔ Put what is said inside **speech marks**.

✔ Put any **punctuation** inside the speech marks, e.g.

'Look out!' said Shasta.

'Why?' asked Tizer.

✔ Use powerful **speech verbs**, e.g. 'Look,' <u>shouted</u> Shasta.

✔ Use 'said' plus an **adverb**, e.g. 'Look,' Shasta said miserably.

✔ Start a **new line** whenever a new speaker speaks.

✔ You can put the speaker **before** or **after** direct speech, e.g. Sandil said, 'When do we arrive?; 'When do we arrive?' asked Sandil.

# Using paragraphs

## Why do we need paragraphs?

Paragraphs help writers to organise their thoughts or ideas. They also make it easier for the reader to follow the storyline.

## How to write in paragraphs

Try building the paragraphs into your plan. Do this by using boxes in a flowchart or a story mountain, where you make each 'part' of the story into a paragraph. In this way a paragraph is rather like a 'scene' in a film. It usually contains one event.

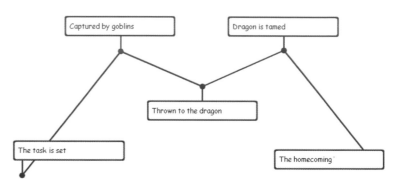

Captured by goblins

Dragon is tamed

Thrown to the dragon

The task is set

The homecoming

## When to change paragraphs

Use this table to help you to work out when a new paragraph is needed:

| When? | Why? | Example |
|---|---|---|
| A new person speaks | To show that it is a different speaker. | 'Hello,' said Daisy. 'Hi there,' replied Poppy, ignoring her. |
| Place | To show that the action has shifted to another place. | In the next room … |
| Time | To let the reader know that time has passed. | The next morning … |
| Person | To introduce a new person or to move the attention to a different character. | The new girl entered; at that moment, Kylie noticed that … |
| Surprising events | This is used when a dramatic, unexpected or exciting event occurs. | There was a crash … |

## WRITER'S TOOLKIT

The main types of paragraph are:

✔ **opening** – set the scene, introduce the main character

✔ **build-up** – get the story going; your character is doing something

✔ **dilemma** – something goes wrong; there is a problem to solve

✔ **resolution** – solving the problem to make everything ok

✔ **ending** – show what has been learned or how a character has changed.

You may also need an action paragraph for the exciting part of the story. A suspense paragraph is also useful to keep the reader on the edge of their seat!

Fiction

## LANGUAGE TOOLKIT

Have you used:

✔ **connectives** to open paragraphs, e.g. Later that day ...

✔ **punchy openings**, e.g. She stopped!

✔ **question openings**, e.g. Was he hurt?

✔ **scene-setters**, e.g. The thunder rumbled.

✔ **character openings**, e.g. Brad banged his head.

✔ **connectives** to link ideas within paragraphs? e.g. as, so, but, after, before, when, while, that, and

# Style

The way in which a story is told is as important as the story itself. Unless your style is lively and interesting, the reader will lose interest.

## Developing your writing style

Good writing style means:

- choosing good words
- varying your sentences.

Remember to link the story together so that the reader can follow what is happening. This means staying in the same tense, using pronouns and connectives.

## Choosing good words

It is worth keeping a writing journal and collecting words to use. Notice well-chosen words when you are reading and store them away. Think about the effect the words have on the meaning. Try to choose words that add something new or unexpected. Try to use powerful language.

## Varying your sentences

Build up a store of different types of sentences. Invent sentences that might be handy for different reasons. Jot these in your writing journal. Notice how good writers vary their sentences. Try copying different sentence patterns and using these in your own writing. Read them aloud and listen to the effect. What do they sound like? Is the meaning powerfully expressed? Try rewriting a sentence to see if you can improve it by using one of the techniques in the table below.

| Technique | How it works | Example |
|---|---|---|
| Questions | To make the reader wonder what has or will happen. | Where was it? |
| Exclamations | To add impact. | Help! |
| Simple sentences | To say what is happening in clear, straightforward language. | The alien winked at me. |
| Compound sentences | To make the writing flow. | The dragon snorted and ate its dinner. |
| Complex sentences | To use when, how or where to add in extra information. | As the dwarf stood up, the sword glowed. |
| Sentence of three for description | To build up a picture in the reader's mind. | He stared at the alien's green boots, golden eyes and purple hands. |
| Sentence of three for action | To speed up the action. | The dragon sneezed, shook its head and then began to cry. |
| Drop in a chunk | To add in information. | Hazza, _hoping he was not late_, ran towards the dragon's den. |
| Tag on a chunk | To add another idea. | Hazza ran towards the dragon's den, _hoping he was not late_. |

## WRITER'S TOOLKIT

Try to vary the **openings** to sentences:

✔ How? – Calmly, she walked on …

✔ Where? – Under the hill was a mine …

✔ When? – After that, they went home …

✔ Use similes, e.g. Like an eagle, he swooped.

✔ Use an 'ing' clause, e.g. Laughing loudly, they …

## LANGUAGE TOOLKIT

Have you used:

✔ precise **nouns**, e.g. Poodle **not** dog

✔ well-chosen **adjectives**, e.g. rusty letter box **not** red letter box

✔ powerful **verbs**, e.g. staggered **not** went

✔ **similes**, e.g. like a giant

✔ **alliteration**, e.g. <u>t</u>rees <u>t</u>ussled

✔ **metaphors**, e.g. cloudy eyes

✔ **personification**, e.g. the moon grinned

✔ **onomatopoeia**? e.g. the wood cracked

# Poetry

## Gather your ideas

Poets find ideas when:

- listening to music
- looking at art or photographs
- day dreaming
- doodling or drawing.

When writing poetry, first of all, you need to decide what you are going to write about. Here are some tips that you might find helpful.

1. If you don't know where to begin, try the following:
   - Look carefully at your subject.
   - Use your memory.
   - Think about what you can see/hear/smell/taste/touch as you look at or think about something.
   - Link two unrelated ideas or objects.

2. Start jotting down words, thoughts and ideas. You could make:
   - notes
   - a word hoard
   - a word list
   - a mind map.

## Organise your ideas

Now you can organise your ideas into a form. Look at the table of different types of poems on page 23.

18

## WRITER'S TOOLKIT

Create pictures in your poems by using:

✔ similes, e.g. *as dark as space; like a moon*

✔ metaphors, e.g. *heart of rock*

Create sounds in your poems by using:

✔ alliteration, e.g. *a snake slipped by*

✔ onomatopoeia, e.g. *bees buzzed*

✔ rhyme for performance, e.g. *got lost/to my cost.*

Revise your writing by:

✔ deleting words          ✔ reorganising words

✔ adding words            ✔ using alliteration/similes, etc.

✔ changing words          ✔ trying different forms.

## LANGUAGE TOOLKIT

Have you used:

✔ precise **nouns**, e.g. — Siamese **not** cat

✔ powerful **verbs**, e.g. — snapped **not** said

✔ well-chosen **adjectives**, e.g. — cracked window/glassy window

✔ well-chosen adverbs, e.g. — cautiously

✔ surprising **word combinations**, e.g. — cockerel lava

✔ **compressed language**, e.g. — thin heron, **not** the heron was thin

✔ **repetition** for effect?

19

# Playscripts

## Where to start?

A play is a story that is performed by actors. You could begin by taking a story that you know well and turning it into a play. Or you might start by putting a character into a situation and seeing what happens. You can begin by improvising a scene and then acting it several times until you have sorted out the words and movements. Try dramatising a poem or short story.

## What sort of play do you want to put on?

Think about how much time you have and where you could perform your play. Decide on the type of performance:

- play
- video
- puppet show
- musical
- radio drama
- sketch.

Decide on the purpose of your play:

- Is it to make the audience laugh or cry?
- Is it to make them understand something?
- Do you want to scare or frighten them?

> ### Remember!
> All audiences will want to be entertained.

Ask yourself if you need:

- scenery
- props
- costumes
- make-up
- lighting
- sound effects.

For more information on planning and structuring your plot, refer to page 10.

For more information on building believable characters, refer to page 6.

For guidance on creating a setting, refer to page 8.

## WRITER'S TOOLKIT

✔ List the characters at the start of the play.

✔ Longer plays are divided into acts, which are separated by intervals. Each act is made up of a number of scenes.

✔ Start by describing the scene and what the characters are doing in italics/brackets. Write this in the present tense as 'stage directions'.

✔ Put the name of the speaker on the left. Use a colon to separate the characters' names from what they say.

✔ Insert occasional character directions to suggest how something should be spoken, especially if it is not obvious.

✔ Put stage directions in italics/brackets to show what characters should do, if it is not obvious but is important.

✔ Dialogue is the most important aspect of a play. It moves the plot forwards, tells you more about the characters, and it can even give information about the setting.

✔ Where possible, include the use of dance, song, music or sound effects.

## LANGUAGE TOOLKIT

✔ Do **not** use speech marks or speech verbs.

✔ Write your play like a **conversation**.

✔ Use **adverb** for directions (angrily, moving swiftly).

✔ Speech may use:
- slang (geddit?)
- contracted forms (don't)
- conversational words (wos up?)
- everyday expressions (don't give me grief).

### Performers' checklist

✔ Speak clearly.

✔ Be loud enough.

✔ Use plenty of expression.

✔ Keep in your 'role'.

✔ Do not stand in front of each other.

✔ Do not talk too quickly.

✔ Use gestures to show how you feel.

# Creating suspense

To make your writing really exciting, try to build up suspense. Let the reader begin to think that something dreadful might happen.

1. **All is well**

   First, put your character into a situation where everything is going well. In this way, you can lull the reader into a false sense of security, thinking that everything is all right, e.g.

   *Hamid wandered down the street, kicking the autumn leaves and crisp packets. He ambled past the post office and turned into Brick Lane, whistling as he went along.*

2. **Suggest that something might be about to happen**

   Introduce some suspense by having your character:
   - hear something unusual or out of place that suggests that something might happen, e.g. *he heard a creak …*
   - see a glimpse of something ominous, e.g. *a figure darted out …*

3. **Build the tension**

   When you are writing a suspense paragraph, try to see what is happening in your mind. It will need to be very 'visual' so the reader can also see what is happening. It helps if you make the scene dark and cold. It also helps if the character is alone. Try using short sentences for drama. Use a question to make the reader wonder what is happening. It is also helpful if you show the main character's reactions.

   *Suddenly, there was a scream. Nervously, Hamid spun round. The street was empty but he could hear the fencing creak. As he stared into the gloom, street lights flickered on. Hamid shivered. Then he saw a figure duck down behind a car. Who was it? Hamid wasn't waiting to find out. He ran.*

## WRITER'S TOOLKIT

✔ Use short sentences, e.g. *Kiri glanced up.*
✔ Use powerful verbs, e.g. *glanced.*
✔ Introduce a glimpse, e.g. *a dark shadow.*
✔ Introduce a sound effect, e.g. *footsteps.*
✔ Use a question to make the reader wonder, e.g. *who was it?*
✔ Use an adverb starter to show how the character feels, e.g. *Fearfully …*

# Story/Poetry types

| Story type | Characters | Settings | Key features |
|---|---|---|---|
| Adventure | Hero, heroine, baddy | Island, cave, tunnel | Cliff hangers, action |
| Fantasy | Dwarf, hobbit, goblin, dragon | Enchanted forest, cloud city, lonely tower, ruined bridge | Magical events, tasks |
| Sci-fi | Alien, space pilot, robot, space creature | Other planets, spaceships, polluted planets, undersea world | New inventions, computers |
| School/home | Teacher, friends, gangs, bully | Playground, classroom, journey to school | Issues, e.g. bullying, stealing, lying |
| Traditional | Princess, king, ogre, magical creatures | Forest, palace, tower, market, cave | Good vs evil, events in in threes, moral at end |

| Poem type | Features |
|---|---|
| Ballad | Formal story, poem or song in rhyming form using verses and chorus. |
| Couplets | Pairs of lines that rhyme or not, e.g. *Tyger, tyger burning bright in the forests of the night.* |
| Performance | Entertaining poem often in rhyme. |
| Rap | Rapid rhyming verse often performed with music. |
| Narrative | Story poem; may rhyme or not, e.g. Chocolate Cake (Michael Rosen); The Highwayman (Alfred Noyes). |
| Nonsense | Invented words, e.g. *squirtle*; fantastical ideas; often rhyming, e.g. *Twas brillig and the slithy toves did gyre and gimble in the wabe.* |
| Lists | Repeated pattern or phrase, e.g. *last night I saw the moon singing, last night I saw the stars dancing.* |
| Shape | Poem written in the shape of the subject. |
| Free verse | Open pattern; adjectives; similes; metaphors; powerful verbs. |
| Haiku | Japanese form; usually three lines; carefully-chosen words, often 5, 7, 5 syllables. |
| Cinquain | Five lines; ending in a surprise, using 2, 4, 6, 8, 2 syllables. |
| Concrete | Shape of poem adds to meaning. |
| Calligram | Letters in shape of words' meaning. |
| Acrostic | Subject used to spell out first, central or end line. |

# Non-fiction writing

There are lots of different kinds of non-fiction texts. In this book you will find **toolkits** to help you remember what to do.

Whenever you write non-fiction, remember to:

- write an **introduction** and make it clear why you are writing
- decide on the best order for your **paragraphs** – this will depend on the task
- start each paragraph with a **topic sentence**
- use relevant **technical language**
- use **accurate descriptions**
- use **connectives**
- write a **conclusion** – this could involve a summing-up, a personal point of view or a general comment.

You can use the toolkits whenever you are writing, for example, literacy, history, geography or science.

# Planning non-fiction writing

You can use the **skeleton diagrams** in this book to help you plan.

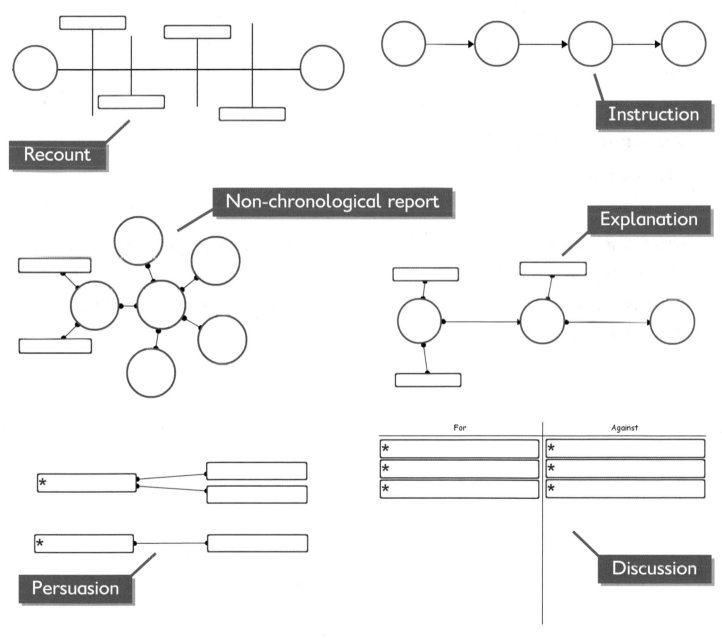

Recount

Instruction

Non-chronological report

Explanation

Persuasion

For

*
*
*

Against

*
*
*

Discussion

The diagrams will help you remember how to organise your writing.

- Add **more words** on the other lines on the diagram to show the facts or examples that you plan to write about. These are memory joggers so you can remember to write about them in detail. **Don't write in sentences**.

- Plan an **introduction** and **conclusion**.

- Think about whether you want to add anything to your writing such as:

  — diagrams

  — fact boxes

  — charts

  — sub-headings.

**Now you are ready to write!**

You can use the pages in this book to help you remember what to do.

Make sure you think about your **purpose** and **audience**. This will affect how you write.

Think about whether your writing will be **formal** or **informal**, or something in between. This will depend on your task and how well you know your audience.

Your writing needs to be **interesting** and **full of detail**.

# Mixed text types

A lot of writing is a **mixture of text types** so you have to decide how to plan.

First decide which **skeleton diagram** will help you **organise** your work most easily.

Then you can think about the different **language features** you need. You may need to look at more than one toolkit.

## Examples

- A **tourist guide** would be planned like a non-chronological report, but it would include persuasive devices to encourage people to visit. Look at how this works in 'Atlantis – a Perfect World' or 'Outer Space, Outer Mind'.

- A **newspaper report** might be mainly recount, but could have sections of explanation to make the detail clear to a reader. It could also be persuasive if the paper was trying to give an opinion about the event. 'The Sinking of the Titanic' is a good example of this.

- A **letter** might contain elements of several text types, depending upon the purpose. Look at the letters sent and received in 'Dispatches from a Quest'.

- A **non-chronological report** might need to include a section of explanation. See how this is done in 'Titanic – the Biggest and Best' or 'The Great White Shark'.

# Writing recounts

**Purpose**

A recount tells us about something that has happened.

**+**

**Audience**

It is for someone who wants to know all about what has happened. The exact audience (and how well you know them) will depend on the task.

There are lots of different kinds of **recount**, for example:

- a write-up of a trip or activity
- an account of something that happened in history
- a newspaper article about something that happened
- a letter to tell someone about an event
- a diary or 'blog' (website diary)
- an encyclopaedia entry
- a biography or autobiography
- an account of a science experiment.

Look at the example below from 'A Visit to Jerusalem'.

## Organisation toolkit

Remember to:

- write a **title** to interest the reader
- write an **introduction** that sets the scene. You could try to answer the questions *who?*, *what?*, *where?*, *when?* and *why?* and convince the reader to read on
- write about events in **paragraphs**, organised in **chronological order**. Choose details that are amusing, exciting or significant in order to interest the reader
- start each paragraph with a **topic sentence**
- write a **conclusion**. This could comment on what happened or say something about how the people involved felt.

## LANGUAGE TOOLKIT

Remember to:

- ✔ write in the **past tense**, except for present circumstances and feelings
- ✔ use **time connecting phrases** (*After the flight; over the first three days of the pilgrimage*)
- ✔ include the **names of people** and **places** (*Father Mark; Bethlehem*)
- ✔ use other **topic words** and examples of relevant **technical language** (*holy water; sermon*)
- ✔ use **accurate descriptions** (*three stone pillars; white cotton cloth*)
- ✔ use either **first person** (personal account) or **third person** (impersonal account)
- ✔ use **direct quotes** and/or **reported speech** where relevant. (*Pat said, 'I had not until then thought of myself as a pilgrim embarking on a pilgrimage, but as just an ordinary person going on a rather special holiday'.*)

Non-fiction

# Writing non-chronological reports

**Purpose**

A report gives factual information about a range of subjects, for example, animals, types of transport, life in Tudor times, towns.

**+**

**Audience**

It is for someone who wants to know about something.

There are lots of different kinds of **report**, for example:

- an information leaflet
- a newspaper or magazine article
- a letter
- a non-fiction book

- an encyclopaedia entry
- a catalogue
- a school website.

Look at this example from 'Great White Shark'.

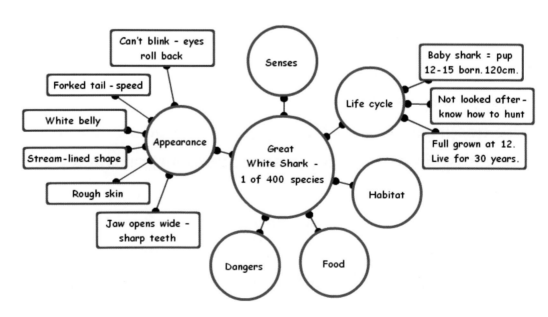

## Organisation toolkit

Remember to:

- write a **title** to say what you are writing about. Try to interest the reader (*Titanic – the Biggest and the Best*)
- write an **introduction** that defines the subject. You should also try to make a statement or ask a question to interest or intrigue the reader so that they want to read on
- organise your work into **paragraphs**, starting with a **topic sentence**. You could also use **sub-headings** to divide up your work
- write your paragraphs in any order, but think about the most sensible order, for example, in a report about an animal, describe the appearance first
- draw **diagrams**, **charts** or **fact boxes** if they help to give the information more clearly
- write a **conclusion** that draws your writing to an end
- include a **glossary** at the end, if relevant.

## LANGUAGE TOOLKIT

Remember to:

- ✔ write in the **present tense** except for historical reports
- ✔ write in the **third person** (*he, she, it, they*)
- ✔ write mainly in a **formal style**, however, you might want to refer directly to the reader at the end
- ✔ use relevant **technical language** (*tenticles, skull, teeth*)
- ✔ use **accurate descriptions** to give information (*white belly, razor sharp teeth*)
- ✔ include **interesting detail** and **several facts or examples** about each part of the subject (*Astounding as it may seem a Great White might lose and replace up to 40,000 teeth during its lifetime*)
- ✔ use '**weasel words**' to cover exceptions (*usually, maybe, generally*).

# Writing instructions

| Purpose | | Audience |
|---|---|---|
| Instructions tell us how to do or make something. | **+** | Instructions are for someone who needs to know how to do or make something. |

There are lots of different kinds of **instructions**. Some need to be written in order, for example:

- a recipe
- an instruction poster, e.g. instructions on how to use a computer
- an instruction leaflet, e.g. on how to make a hand puppet or safety instructions on an aeroplane
- instructions for a game
- map directions.

Some **instructions** do not need to be written in order, for example:

- a list of school rules
- a poster showing advice on water safety.

Look at the example below from 'Air Safety'.

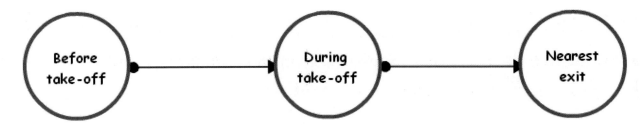

## Organisation toolkit

Remember to:

- write a **title** that sets out the purpose for the instructions (*Safety Instructions*)
- if relevant, write an **opening** sentence directed at the reader (*Follow these instructions to ensure proper safety*)
- include lists of **equipment** or **ingredients**, if needed
- write the instructions as a **sequence of steps**
- use **bullet points** or **numbers** to make the order clear
- draw **diagrams** if they help to give the information more clearly
- write an **ending** sentence directed at the reader. (*Enjoy your flight with Flyaway Airlines.*)

## LANGUAGE TOOLKIT

Remember to:

- ✔ use **imperative verbs** (<u>Put</u> *seats into the upright position*)
- ✔ use the **present tense** and **third person** for instructions
- ✔ use some **time connectives** (*first, next*)
- ✔ use **technical language** related to the subject (*emergency exit, aisle*)
- ✔ use **accurate descriptions** in order to make the instructions clear (*Insert the <u>metal</u> tab into the buckle*).

# Writing explanations

<table>
<tr><td>

**Purpose**

An explanation states **how** or **why** something happens, or **how** something works.

</td><td>

**+**

</td><td>

**Audience**

It is for someone who wants to understand something.

</td></tr>
</table>

There are lots of different kinds of **explanations**. Some are complete texts and others are parts of a mixed text, for example:

- a question and answer leaflet
- a section of explanation in a letter or newspaper article
- a non-fiction book
- an encyclopaedia entry
- a conclusion to a science experiment
- a technical manual, such as for a computer or game console.

Look at the example below from 'Jet Engine'.

## Organisation toolkit

Remember to:

- write a **title** to say what you are writing about (*The Jet Engine – how does it work?*)
- write an **introduction** to give any background information
- write your **paragraphs** in **chronological order**. Start each new section with a **topic sentence**
- draw **a diagram** if it helps make your explanation clearer
- use **bullet points** or **sub-headings** if this helps break up the explanation
- write a **conclusion** that relates the subject to the reader, if possible.

## LANGUAGE TOOLKIT

Remember to:

✔ write in the **present tense**, unless you are writing an explanation about something in the past

✔ write in the **third person** (*it, they*)

✔ use **a formal** style

✔ use **time connectives** to show the order clearly (*first, next, then*)

✔ use words to show **how** or **why** (**cause and effect**) (*because, consequently, therefore, when*)

✔ use **technical vocabulary**. Define any difficult words or include them in a **glossary** (*thrust, nozzle*)

✔ use **clear descriptions** to help explain things

✔ use 'weasel words' to cover generalisations (*usually, often*)

✔ make the explanation **interesting** for the reader.

# Writing persuasion

<table>
<tr><td>

**Purpose**

Persuasive writing is for arguing a case for a point of view.

</td><td>

**+**

</td><td>

**Audience**

It is for anyone who might be interested in the subject, but may have a different point of view. This means you have to include lots of facts and arguments to try to make them agree with you.

</td></tr>
</table>

There are lots of different kinds of **persuasive writing**, for example:

- an advertisement
- a poster or flier
- a book 'blurb'
- a newspaper or magazine article
- a leaflet, e.g. from people who want to stop whale hunting)
- a letter, e.g. from someone trying to persuade somebody to do something).

Look at the example below from 'Dolphins'.

## Organisation toolkit

Remember to:

- write an **eye-catching** title to say what you are writing about, (*Protect the Dolphin Before its Too Late*)
- write an **introduction** that states the point of view to be argued
- write your points in **paragraphs**, starting with **topic sentences**. These signal the argument to be made in that paragraph
- think about what your opponents might argue and include **counter arguments**. You can either do this in each paragraph as you go along or in a paragraph at the end
- use **bullet points**, **sub-headings** and **pictures** if these help to make your points clearer or stronger
- write an **ending** that re-states your point of view.

## LANGUAGE TOOLKIT

Remember to:

- ✔ write in the **present tense**
- ✔ choose **emotive language** to help give your point of view (<u>Thousands of</u> dolphins are <u>cruelly trapped</u> in fishing nets each year)
- ✔ use words to give **reasons** for your point of view (*because, so, this means that*)
- ✔ use 'dare-to-disagree' expressions to get the reader on your side. Try to appear friendly and reasonable (*There is no doubt; the time has come to INSIST that all countries pass laws to protect them from harm*)
- ✔ use type **size** and **punctuation** for effect
- ✔ use **technical vocabulary** (*tuna fishing, trawling, nets*)
- ✔ use **connecting phrases** to signal your points (<u>In addition</u>, *action needs to be taken because dolphins are in great danger*)
- ✔ use **alliteration** and **rhyme** if it helps the task
- ✔ use **'weasel words'** to help persuade (*probably, perhaps, often*).

# Writing discussion

## Purpose

A discussion puts forward both sides of the argument. It gives points **for** and **against** as a **balanced** piece of writing.

**+**

## Audience

It is for anyone who is interested in the subject. They might be trying to make up their mind by reading what you have written.

There are lots of different kinds of **discussion writing**, for example:

- a leaflet about both sides of an issue
- a newspaper article
- information in non-fiction books
- a write-up of a debate.

Look at the example from 'Loch Ness'.

### Does the Loch Ness monster exist?

| For (Nicky) | Against (Adam) |
| --- | --- |
| ✶ Sightings & photos | ✶ Sightings & photos |
| ✶ Expedition | ✶ No scientific proof |
| ✶ Don't have to see to believe | ✶ Conditions in loch |

## Organisation toolkit

Remember to:

- write a **title** to say what you are writing about (*Jet Travel – cut or keep it?*)
- write an **introduction** that states what the discussion is about (*There are many stories of sightings of a monster in Loch Ness in Scotland. However people disagree about whether it exists or not*)
- organise the main part of the discussion in one of two ways:
  1. First write about all the arguments **for** the case. Write one **paragraph** for each point and begin each new point with a **topic sentence**. The write about the arguments **against** the case. Write one **paragraph** for each point and begin each new point with a **topic sentence**
  2. Present each argument and counter argument in a separate **paragraph**, which starts with a **topic sentence**
- write a **conclusion** that sums up the argument and gives a reasoned opinion.

## LANGUAGE TOOLKIT

Remember to:

✔ write in the **present tense**
✔ write in the **third** person
✔ use **technical vocabulary** (*pollution, greenhouse gases, climate change*)
✔ use words to show **reasons** (*because, so*)
✔ use **descriptions** to help make the facts clear
✔ use words to signal **both sides** of the argument (*on the one hand enviornmentalists point out, some people argue, others believe, however supporters of the monster theory say*)
✔ use **connecting phrases** to signal your points (*first of all, in addition*)
✔ use 'weasel words' to help back up a point (*probably, perhaps, often*)
✔ give **examples** to back up what you say.

Non-fiction

# Writing letters

## Purpose

There are lots of reasons for writing a letter, for example, to keep in touch with someone, to send news, to complain, to congratulate, to persuade, to reply to a previous letter, to ask for information or to explain something.

Letters can involve different **text types**. This means you will need to use parts of the other **toolkits** in this book to help you write your letter.

+

## Audience

Your audience could be a friend or relation (a **personal** letter) or someone you don't know (a **formal** letter).

Look at the examples below of a personal letter and a formal letter from 'Dispatches from a Quest'.

## Personal letter

Dear Bramble,

Thog and I have been travelling for so long that we can hardly remember what home looks like any more.
First we had to cross the great mountains. There we got caught in a blizzard. It was so cold that I thought we would not survive.

Look after my hens and whatever happens, do not let anyone else steal my old tinder box.

Your friend - Nat the hen keeper

## Formal letter

Dear Sir,

I am writing to complain about the items that I bought from your shop last moon-month.

I will be calling at your shop once this adventure is over and expect a refund for these goods.

Yours sincerely,
Nat Treegood

## Organisation toolkit for a personal letter

Remember to:

- write **your address** in the **top right** hand part of the page
- write the **date** underneath the address
- start your letter on the **left** hand side of the page. Use an informal greeting (*Dear Bramble*)
- explain why you are writing in the **first sentence**
- set out your letter in **paragraphs**. Start each one on a new line with a **topic sentence**
- **sign off** your letter on a new line
- make your letter **detailed and interesting**.

## Organisation toolkit for a formal letter

Remember to:

- write **your address** in the **top right** hand part of the page
- write the **date** underneath the address
- write the **address** of the person the letter is for. Write this lower down than the date and on the **left** hand side of the page
- start your letter underneath with a **formal** greeting (*Dear Sir*)
- explain **who** you are and **why** you are writing in the **first sentence**
- set out your letter in **paragraphs**. Start each one on a new line with a **topic sentence**
- write about what you want to happen next in your **closing paragraph**
- sign off your letter on a new line (*Yours sincerely*).

## LANGUAGE TOOLKIT

Remember to:

✔ write in a **formal** style
✔ make your letter **clear** and **detailed**.

# Writing diaries

**Purpose**
A diary is for recording events, thoughts and feelings for now and in the future.

**+**

**Audience**
It is usually just for the writer. However, sometimes a diary is read by other people, for example, *Anne Frank's Diary.*

A diary is a **recount**. Remember all the points on the **toolkits** on page 29 and look at the extra toolkits below.

**Organisation toolkit**
Remember to:
- write the **date** (and possibly the time) at the start of each entry
- organise your writing into **paragraphs**. These should show the sequence of events and the flow of your thoughts.

## LANGUAGE TOOLKIT

Remember to:
- ✔ use the **past tense** to record events and the **present tense** for thoughts and feelings (*I am so excited because ...*)
- ✔ use an **informal style**
- ✔ use **powerful** and **emotive** words and phrases to show your own thoughts and reactions
- ✔ choose words carefully to make **links** between diary entries. (*It is five weeks now since ...*)

# Biographical writing

## Purpose
**Autobiographies** record the life of the author. **Biographies** record someone else's life.

## Audience
Both kinds of writing are for people who are interested in finding out more about the person.

Autobiographies and biographies are examples of **recounts**.

Look at the **toolkits** on page 29 and the extra toolkits lists below.

## Organisation toolkit
Remember to:
- write an **introduction** that makes the person sound interesting or unusual
- include family trees, timelines, photographs or pictures with captions
- write a **conclusion** that contains a reflection on the person's life or (if the person is still alive) some hopes or thoughts about the future.

## LANGUAGE TOOLKIT

### Autobiography
Remember to:
- ✔ write in the **first person**
- ✔ include your **opinions** and **feelings**
- ✔ choose whether to write in a **formal** or **informal** style
- ✔ include **quotes** from people who know you, in direct or reported speech.

### Biography
Remember to:
- ✔ write in the **third person**
- ✔ write in a **formal** style
- ✔ include **quotes** from people who knew the person, in direct or reported speech.

# Journalistic writing

The purpose and audience for **journalistic writing** depends upon the kind of article being written and the type of newspaper or magazine it is published in.

> **Purpose**
>
> Newspapers and magazines keep people up to date with news events, provide entertainment and tell people more about subjects that interest them.

**+**

> **Audience**
>
> Newspapers and magazines usually have a specific **target audience**.

Examples of target audiences:

- A local newspaper is for people who live in a certain area.
- A school newspaper is for everyone connected with the school.
- Magazines about different topics (for example, computer games, model-making, music, cooking, gardening) are for people who like these activities.
- Comics are usually for children.

Newspapers and magazines contain:

- news stories
- interviews
- letters
- advertisements
- puzzles
- reports.

Many articles are **mixed text types**.

> **THE DAILY TIMES**
> April 17th 1912
>
> **TITANIC HAS SUNK!**
> At 11.40pm on April 14th, the world's largest ocean liner skimmed the side of an iceberg in the Atlantic Ocean. Three hours later she had sunk. Over 1500 people have drowned or been frozen to death in the icy waters.

## Organisation toolkit

Remember to:

- include a **masthead** (name of paper), the **date** and a **headline**
- include a **flash** (a one line summary of the contents of the page)
  (Over 1500 passengers died when Titanic hit an iceberg)
- give an **introduction** to sum up the story and interest the reader.
  This is often in **bold** type
- write in **columns** and use **sub-headings**
- include **pictures** with **captions** and **diagrams**, if relevant
- give a **conclusion** that might include the paper's opinion
- include a **by-line** (the reporter's name).

## LANGUAGE TOOLKIT

Remember to:

- ✔ write in the **third** person
- ✔ use attention-grabbing language such as powerful **verbs** and **adjectives**, emotive language and short, snappy phrases
- ✔ use **alliteration**, **rhyme**, **puns** and **word play** in the headlines (*Fall of the Titan*)
- ✔ include **quotations** from people who saw what happened as **direct** or **indirect speech** (*Eye witnesses report that as the bow section sank, the stern righted itself for a short time*)
- ✔ use standard phrases for anything that is uncertain (*Mr Smith claimed; it is alleged*).

# Informal writing

An **informal style** is rather like conversation. It can be used in:

- diary writing
- letters to friends
- some kinds of persuasive writing such as adverts, fliers and personal opinions
- notes to yourself.

Look at the example from 'Guide to Planet Marco'.

**Top of the World**

Are you the outdoor type? Do you like to challenge yourself? Get away from the daily routine and travel to one of the most beautiful places in the universe with this tailor-made Mountain Trek on Planet Marco, the red planet.

The spectacular Morstan Mountain Range is one of the great wonders of the universe. The mountains tower more than several miles high but the air is always sweet and breathable. Local guides will lead you through this once-in-a-lifetime journey.

Next >

© Planet Marco Tourist Information    NOTE: SITE STILL UNDER CONSTRUCTION!

## LANGUAGE TOOLKIT

Remember to:

✔ use **colloquial words** and **phrases**

✔ make it sound more like **speech**

✔ make use of **punctuation**, for example, use a dash to show an afterthought or an aside.

# Formal writing

A **formal style** is used in many kinds of non-fiction writing, for example:

- explanations
- some non-chronological reports
- some pieces of persuasive writing
- discussions
- business letters.

One of the most important factors in deciding whether to use a formal style is to think about the **task** you are writing and **who** the writing is for. For example, if you are writing to a chairman of a company about a serious complaint, you will need to write formally.

When you write in a formal style, you create a 'distance' between yourself and the reader.

## LANGUAGE TOOLKIT

Remember to:

- ✔ use the **third person**
- ✔ use the **passive voice** to alter the emphasis in the sentence
- ✔ choose more **formal connectives** (*furthermore, nevertheless, moreover, in addition*)
- ✔ use **formal vocabulary** (*enquire/request (ask), respond/response (reply), feature/factor (thing)*)
- ✔ write in a way that avoids personal involvement
- ✔ use **stock phrases** that are 'polite' even though you may be annoyed.

Always think about what you are writing and who is going to read it.

You will often need to decide which features to use in order to write in the correct style for the task.

# Editing writing

1.  Think about the **writing task**.

    - What sort of writing is it?

    - Who is it for?

    - Have you done what you were asked to do?

    - Will your reader understand it?

2.  Look at ways to **improve your sentences**, for example:

    - make words count by changing weak verbs or adjectives

    - make sure that you have a range of sentence types, for example, simple, compound and complex

    - check that you have started sentences in different ways

    - check that you have found different ways of connecting your sentences and ideas

    - edit clumsy sentences, for example, use one word instead of several.

3.  Check your **spelling** and **punctuation**. (It is often easier to spot mistakes if you read your work aloud.)